No, Sid, No!

Written by Kate Scott
Illustrated by Pedro Penizzotto

Collins

Sid sits.

2

Sid is sad.

Sid is mad.

No, Sid, no!

Run, cat, run!

No, Sid! Not the socks!

Sid kicks the mop.

The cat rips the rug.

It is Mum!

Mum is mad.

Sid is sad.

Sid sits.

15

Ideas for reading

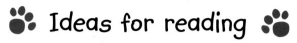

Written by Clare Dowdall, PhD
Lecturer and Primary Literacy Consultant

Learning objectives: read simple words by sounding out and blending the phonemes all through the word from left to right; read a range of familiar and common words and simple sentences independently; extend their vocabulary, exploring the meanings and sounds of new words; retell narratives in the correct sequence, drawing on the language patterns of stories; use language to imagine and recreate roles and experiences

Curriculum links: Knowledge and Understanding of the World: Exploration and investigation

Focus phonemes: r, u, o, d, ck, k, g

Fast words: no, the

Word count: 39

Getting started

- Revise reading the fast words using flash cards.

- Read the title. Discuss the use of the exclamation mark and how to read the second *No!* with emphasis.

- Look at the picture on the front cover together. Ask children to describe what the dog is doing. Discuss who has a dog and what they do that is naughty.

- Read the blurb together. Help children to say the sounds in the right order, blend the sounds and reread each sentence fluently.

Reading and responding

- Read pp2–3 together. Challenge children to add sound buttons to each word and blend to read.

- Discuss why Sid is sad on p3 and what might happen next.

- Ask children to read to p13 aloud. Encourage them to blend phonemes to read new words and to use expression in their voice.

- Listen as children read. Praise children for blending through words and rereading for fluency.